FAMOUS MOVIE MONSTERS™

MEET DRACULA

The Rosen Publishing Group, Inc.
New York

CHARLES HOFER

To Maxwell

Published in 2005 by The Rosen Publishing Group, Inc.
29 East 21st Street, New York, NY 10010

First Edition

Library of Congress Cataloging-in-Publication Data

Hofer, Charles.
Meet Dracula / Charles Hofer.—1st ed.
    p. cm.—(Famous movie monsters)
Includes filmography.
Includes bibliographical references and index.
ISBN 1-4042-0267-6
1. Dracula films—History and criticism—Juvenile literature. 2. Dracula, Count (Fictitious character)—Juvenile literature. I. Title. II. Series.
PN1995.9.D64H64 2005
791.43'651—dc22

                                                          2004008425

Manufactured in the United States of America

On the cover: Dracula (Bela Lugosi, *right*) attempts to bite into the neck of his victim (Helen Chandler) in a still from *Dracula*.

CONTENTS

CHAPTER 1

DRACULA

High in the Carpathian Mountains of Romania, real estate agent R. M. Renfield rides in a swiftly moving carriage along the last leg of his journey. Renfield is visiting this strange land from London at the request of a mysterious nobleman who has expressed interest in buying a home in England. Renfield carries with him a lease for Carfax Abbey, a London estate the Romanian nobleman intends to buy.

Night is falling in Transylvania. The sun is quickly dipping behind a dark forest, and the creatures of the night have begun to stir.

At the village he just left, the townspeople begged Renfield not to continue his journey.

"You mustn't go there," they pleaded. "At the castle there are vampires!"

But Renfield refused to listen. After all, vampires are just superstition.

At Borgo Pass, Renfield exits his carriage. The driver quickly throws Renfield's luggage to the ground and drives off in a hurry to get out of the forest before nightfall. At the pass waits another carriage, one that will bring Renfield to his destination— the castle of Count Dracula.

Bela Lugosi (Dracula) and Dwight Frye (R. M. Renfield) are pictured in this still from *Dracula*. Both actors received critical acclaim for their roles but would ultimately be typecast for the rest of their careers. Lugosi went on to star in many vampire films, while Frye was cast as Dr. Frankenstein's assistant in *Frankenstein*.

Renfield approaches the new carriage. He eyes the driver who sits atop the carriage, his face hidden in shadow.

"C-Coach for Count Dracula?" Renfield asks the driver. There is no reply, just a slow nod.

With caution, Renfield boards the carriage. The driver races away, back through Borgo Pass from where the carriage had come. Before long, the carriage arrives at the castle. Renfield gets out and immediately notices something most peculiar. The driver has disappeared! It is as if the carriage drove itself.

Confused, Renfield stands before Dracula's castle. Stone towers rise high above him, casting a silhouette against the moonlit sky. He slowly climbs the steps to the castle. As he approaches the doors, they open slowly, by themselves. Renfield walks in, taking in the grand entranceway covered in cobwebs and lit by flickering candlelight.

As he is taking in his surroundings, Renfield notices the dark shape of a man emerge from the shadows and approach him. The man is dressed in black; a long cape flows over his shoulders to the floor. His skin is ghostly white, his eyes lifeless.

"I am . . . Dracula," says the man in a thick Romanian accent. A sinister smile breaks across his face. "I bid you . . . welcome."

For a moment, Renfield is relieved, happy at last to have found the Count, his order of business. The Count leads Renfield through the castle to a room where a meal has been set at a table.

The Count and his guest discuss business. Dracula reviews Renfield's papers, the lease to Carfax Abbey, a home in London. The Count nods in agreement, pleased with the lease. He then informs his guest that a ship has been arranged for a passage to England. They will depart in the morning. Dracula leaves Renfield, who dines alone. Renfield enjoys a glass of wine. But he soon feels sleepy, as if the wine he drank was drugged. For him, the night drifts off into darkness.

*   *   *

A wicked storm has risen from the west, and the cargo ship *Vesta* is tossed about in a maddened sea. Below the deck of the ship, a man slinks about the dark galley. His clothes are torn and his hair is strewn about. Several large wooden boxes lie about the ship. The man approaches one box and he leans his head close to it with eyes blazing mad. "Master," he whispers, "you will keep your promise once we reach London? Lives! Small ones with blood in them!"

The dawn finds the *Vesta* wrecked on the shores of Whitby Harbor, south of London. Authorities have gathered on board the mysterious ship. They cannot find any clues as to why the ship has crashed. The crew is nowhere to be found. It is almost as if it has vanished. Only the lifeless body of the captain remains, lashed to the ship's wheel with rope. The only living soul left on board is a raving madman—R. M. Renfield.

*　　*　　*

That evening, the streets of London are crowded with theatergoers. Among them is a well-dressed, caped figure. Count Dracula walks among the Londoners. Amid the crowd, police whistles ring out. In a darkened alley, a young girl lies lifeless, drained of her blood.

Dracula blends into the crowd of people who flow into a theater to see a performance. In the balcony, Count Dracula meets Dr. Jack Seward, who runs the sanatorium adjacent to Carfax Abbey, the Count's new home. The Count introduces himself to Seward's guests: Seward's daughter Mina, her fiancé Jonathan Harker, and Mina's friend, Lucy Weston. The mysterious Count fascinates the group and they look forward to getting to know their new neighbor. Likewise, the Count is immediately struck by young Lucy's beauty.

The following morning, Lucy has fallen sick. She is weak and pale. Dr. Seward takes care of her, but he cannot find a reason for her illness. He can only determine that she has lost a considerable amount of blood and that there are two small punctures on her neck. Besides these indications, there is no explanation for her affliction.

As her health gets worse by the hour, Dr. Seward decides there is only one thing left to do. He must summon his friend Professor Abraham Van Helsing, a brilliant man from the East who specializes in mysterious ailments.

By the time Van Helsing arrives at Lucy's bedside, it is too late. Lucy is dead. Van Helsing inspects Lucy's body and runs tests to find some explanation. He is perplexed by the sudden ailment, but something is turning in his mind. Could it really be?

That afternoon, Van Helsing calls a meeting with Dr. Seward and Jonathan Harker. He has come to a conclusion about Lucy's death. It is the only possible explanation, he decides. He looks slowly over his hosts, trying to determine how they will respond to his words. "Gentlemen," the professor begins, "we are dealing with the undead. Nosferatu—the vampire."

Dr. Seward is stunned. "But vampires are pure myth!" he cries in disbelief. "A superstition!"

Van Helsing is confident. He has seen it before: the sudden weakness, the unexplained loss of blood, the two marks on the victim's neck. There is no other explanation—a vampire is haunting London.

Dracula (Bela Lugosi) stealthily approaches the sleeping Mina Seward (Helen Chandler) to feast on her blood. Despite the sharp teeth that later became associated with the character of Dracula, no fangs are actually visible in the 1931 film, nor is the famous vampire bite mark shown on Dracula's victims.

*   *   *

That evening, in a cavern far below Carfax Abbey, a large wooden coffin slowly opens. A tall figure dressed in black emerges. Dracula, the undead, has risen for the evening. He will feast on the blood of the living.

The next morning, Mina awakens. She, too, is weakened and pale, just as Lucy was two days before. Van Helsing is called in to inspect her. As Jonathan comforts Mina, she

explains that she had terrible dreams of a large bat hovering outside her window. In the dream she saw two glowing eyes— evil eyes—approaching her. When she awoke, she felt ill, weakened, drained of life.

Van Helsing asks her to remove the scarf that covers her neck. There he finds two small marks on her neck, just as he suspected. The professor's eyes fall. Now there is no doubt.

Jonathan desperately pleads with Van Helsing, "What could have caused them?"

"Count Dracula!" announces the maid suddenly. The group turns to the entranceway as the Count walks into the room.

As Van Helsing is introduced to the Count, a chill runs down Van Helsing's spine. The Count looks equally suspiciously at Van Helsing, almost as if they've met before.

Dracula approaches Mina and inquires about her affliction and assures her that she will soon be back to normal. Meanwhile, from across the room, the professor picks up a cigarette box. He raises the lid, which contains a mirror that reflects the image behind him. In the mirror, Van Helsing sees Mina sitting on the couch, talking to someone, but no one is there. He turns to look at Mina. She is clearly sitting on the couch, speaking to the Count who stands next to her. He returns his gaze to the reflected image. Again, he sees only Mina, talking to the empty space. Van Helsing slowly closes the box and smiles.

Dracula and Mina walk through the shadowy woods together. One of *Dracula*'s major assets is the spooky sets Universal created for the film. Though the production was not as lavish as originally intended, due to the economic crunch of the Great Depression, the menacing woods and Gothic architecture used for the sets created a memorable look of terror befitting the horrifying tale.

Meanwhile, Dracula has finished soothing Mina. He turns to leave, but Van Helsing blocks his path. Van Helsing carries the cigarette box toward the Count. "A moment ago, I stumbled upon a most amazing phenomenon," he tells Dracula. Just then he opens the box, capturing Dracula in the mirror. Dracula's eyes rage in horror as he looks into the mirror. With a swift blow he strikes the box, shattering it to pieces.

Dracula's cold eyes slowly descend on the professor. A look of fury fills his ghostly face. A dead silence fills the room.

Slowly, Dracula turns to the professor and smiles, "For someone who has not lived a single lifetime, you are a wise man, Van Helsing." The Count then tips his hat to his hosts, turns, and leaves.

On the couch, Jonathan is holding his fiancée, trying desperately to comfort her. Dr. Seward approaches the professor to learn the meaning of the scene with the Count.

Van Helsing confidently announces, "Dracula is our vampire."

*   *   *

Later, in the middle of the night, a maid's horrible scream breaks the house's midnight silence.

"Mina's out there—dead!" she cries.

Van Helsing and Dr. Seward run out to the courtyard where they find Mina's body. She is still alive, but barely.

Once inside the house, the professor and Dr. Seward discuss the situation. "Alive, yes," says the professor. "But she's in greater danger, for she's already under his influence." Mina has fallen under Dracula's spell, he explains. It is only a matter of time before she, too, becomes one of the undead.

While Mina is brought to her room, Van Helsing meets with Jonathan and Dr. Seward. "The only thing we can do to save Mina's life," Van Helsing says, "is to find the hiding place of Dracula's living corpse and drive a stake through his heart!"

Renfield, a patient at Dr. Seward's sanatorium, runs to Carfax Abbey to warn Dracula. Van Helsing and Jonathan follow Renfield to Carfax Abbey. The old house is shrouded in shadows. The two watch Renfield enter an opening in the caverns below the abbey. As they watch him ascend the steep staircase, Dracula and Mina are descending the stairs. Jonathan calls out Mina's name, revealing their presence. Dracula carries Mina into the shadows of the caverns below.

The caverns are lit dimly by flickering candlelight. Van Helsing and Jonathan quickly search for Dracula's coffin. Soon they stumble across a vaulted, cryptlike room full of wooden boxes. Van Helsing approaches a large box and breaks open its lid. There lies Dracula in a lifeless sleep. But Mina is not beside him!

Van Helsing knows there is no time to lose. Soon the Count will rise to feast on the living. Van Helsing grabs a splintered piece of the coffin lid. He yells to Jonathan to find something to serve as a hammer. After a moment Jonathan returns with a large stone. Van Helsing places the stake of wood on Dracula's chest, then raises the stone and quickly brings it down upon the stake. It drives through the heart of the vampire.

As the stake passes through Dracula, a slight scream pierces the darkness. "Mina!" cries Jonathan. He rushes to the shadows to find his love. She is weak and shaken, but she is finally released from Dracula's wicked curse.

CHAPTER 2

DRACULA ON THE SILVER SCREEN

The 1931 movie *Dracula* hypnotized filmgoers around the world. *Dracula* was based on the novel of the same name, which was written by Irishman Bram Stoker and published in 1897. Never before had Hollywood produced such a lavish and terrifying tale. Critics praised it, and the public returned again and again to relive the encounter with the blood-thirsty Count Dracula.

The success of *Dracula* sparked an explosion of monster movies whose popularity lasted generations. Count Dracula would be reproduced in dozens of films, creating an industry of vampire movies.

NOSFERATU

Nearly a decade before American audiences would glimpse Count Dracula for the first time, a strangely familiar tale of horror appeared in cinemas in Germany. In 1922, Prana Films, a German film company, had hopes of making a splash with its first silent film, *Nosferatu*.

Max Schreck starred in *Nosferatu* as the title character, a vampire modeled on Count Dracula. Though the 1922 film's striking similarity to Bram Stoker's novel caused controversy and provoked a lawsuit from Stoker's widow, *Nosferatu* struck a chord with audiences and proved the popularity of the vampire tale. However, because of the controversy surrounding the movie, it would be almost a decade until Universal produced *Dracula*.

The film's plot is remarkably similar to Stoker's novel. However, the producers altered the storyline to avoid buying rights to the novel. They set the story in Germany, changed characters' names, and modified the plot. This strategy did not work and eventually caused a controversy. The story was much too similar to Stoker's novel and infringed on copyright laws. Upon release of the film, Stoker's widow, Florence

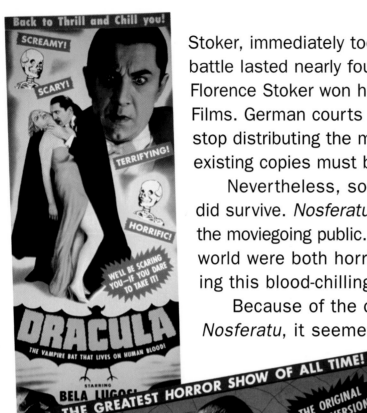

Stoker, immediately took legal action. The legal battle lasted nearly four years, and, in the end, Florence Stoker won her case against Prana Films. German courts ordered the company to stop distributing the movie and ruled that all existing copies must be destroyed.

Nevertheless, some copies of the movie did survive. *Nosferatu* had cast its spell over the moviegoing public. Theatergoers around the world were both horrified and thrilled at seeing this blood-chilling tale brought to life.

Because of the controversy surrounding *Nosferatu*, it seemed as though the story of Dracula would forever be locked away, never to appear in film—at least in Hollywood. In the mid-1920s, however, Dracula appeared again—this time on the stage.

Movie posters for *Dracula* showcase a menacing Bela Lugosi as the Count. The Hungarian actor's eerie delivery of dialogue was a result of not knowing English very well, and he was therefore forced to learn his lines phonetically.

DRACULA MAKES IT TO BROADWAY

By the mid-1920s, *Dracula* fever had a grip on the London theater scene. Audience members fainted during showings. Nurses were assigned to the theater to assist stricken theater-goers. One night, legendary theater producer and publisher Horace Liveright attended a showing of *Dracula* at a London theater. What Liveright saw was the story's potential to both captivate and horrify audiences. He realized he had to bring the Count to America.

In 1927, *Dracula* arrived on New York City's Broadway. The Broadway adaptation starred a little-known Hungarian actor named Bela Lugosi as the Count. Lugosi fell into the role and developed a suave yet revolting version of the Dark Prince. The play was a resounding success and ran for several seasons. By 1930, no one could deny the popularity and magnetism of Stoker's Count Dracula. From Broadway, there was only one place left to go—Hollywood, California.

DRACULA HEADS WEST

The 1930s ushered in the golden age of Hollywood, and the possibilities seemed limitless. The age of the silent film had drawn to a close. The new "talkies" were the favorite in Hollywood. Moviegoers could now hear what the actors were saying. Sound effects were used, and music was added for dramatic effect. The silver screen seemed perfect for *Dracula*.

After long negotiations, Florence Stoker sold the film rights to *Dracula*. The rights were sold to Universal Studios, one of the largest film studios in Hollywood. Universal knew it had a winner with *Dracula*. The studio made *Dracula*'s production a priority, giving it the status of a "Universal Super Production."

CREATING THE COUNT

Preproduction on *Dracula* began in early 1930 and was led by producer Carl Laemmle. The picture was awarded a budget of $355,000. Pulitzer Prize–winning writer and Hollywood newcomer Louis Bromfield was hired to pen the movie's script. Next, the studio hired the notorious director Tod Browning, who had already made several successful silent films for Universal. He also had a reputation of being a heavy drinker and someone with whom it was difficult to work. But hiring Browning was part of a larger design by studio executives. Previously, Browning had directed successful movies such as *The Unholy Three* (1925) and *London After Midnight* (1927). These movies starred the great actor Lon Chaney, known as the Man of a Thousand Faces. Chaney was an immensely popular star in Hollywood at the time. He was famous for bringing to life horribly dark and twisted characters in such pictures as *The Hunchback of Notre Dame* (1923) and *The*

Lon Chaney, shown here in *The Phantom of the Opera* (1925), made a name for himself in horror movies throughout the 1920s. He was Universal's original choice to play Dracula. However, the actor died of cancer before production began on the movie.

Director Tod Browning (*center, standing*) poses with the cast of *Freaks* (1932), a film set in the world of sideshow performers that was banned in England and many parts of the United States. Though Browning enjoyed great success with *Dracula*, he saw his reputation as an A-list director diminish through the 1930s.

Phantom of the Opera (1925). With Browning directing Chaney as the Count, Universal was almost guaranteed a box-office sensation.

Unfortunately, this magical pairing was not meant to be. Chaney died of cancer before production of *Dracula* even began. With the movie already in preproduction in mid-1930, Universal was without a Count Dracula.

Financial problems slowed preproduction as well. The United States' economy was still reeling from the stock market crash of 1929. Originally the movie was planned as a

BELA LUGOSI

Few actors have left such an indelible mark on Hollywood as Bela Lugosi. Lugosi's Hungarian accent, dramatic gestures, and cold eyes made him the perfect actor to bring the bloodthirsty Count to life. His role in *Dracula* was a resounding success and assured Lugosi a place as a Hollywood legend. But it would be a terrible price to pay. For the rest of his life, the shadow of Count Dracula would loom over Lugosi's career.

Lugosi was born Bela Ferenc Dezso Blasko in 1882 in Lugos, Hungary (today's Lugoj, Romania). He began his acting career in European theaters, moved to the United States in 1921, and first gained attention there while playing the lead role in the stage production of *Dracula*. After the release of the film *Dracula*, Lugosi shot to Hollywood fame. As the monster-movie genre gained popularity, so did Lugosi. Over the years, he battled Boris Karloff (of *Frankenstein* fame) for recognition as the most popular movie monster. Although the success of *Dracula* made him a star, Lugosi's career as a serious actor was ruined. He had been typecast and would never be able to escape the curse of Count Dracula. For the rest of his career, Lugosi would play some horrible and twisted characters, sad spin-offs of the Count he had made famous. He even reprised his role as the Count in the classic 1948 comedy *Abbott and Costello Meet Frankenstein*. Eventually his career all but dried up. By 1950, Lugosi was mired in depression and a morphine addiction. In 1956, Lugosi died while filming Ed Wood's classic B film *Plan 9 from Outer Space*. According to the request of his will, Lugosi was buried wearing the cape of Count Dracula.

The Count opens his cape to draw in Mina, his beautiful young victim, in *Dracula*. Although Lugosi was not Universal's first choice to play Dracula, he was perhaps the most well prepared actor for the role, having spent years playing the character on stage in the Broadway version. His utterly convincing incarnation of the Count haunted him for the rest of his career, as he wound up being typecast in many vampire movies.

large-scale, lavish film. But Universal was feeling the economic crunch and had to streamline production. This would move the film's storyline away from Stoker's complex novel and closer to the more practical Broadway show.

By the summer of 1930, many of the actors had already been cast. David Manners, a rising young Canadian actor, was cast as Jonathan Harker. Actors Edward Van Sloan (as Professor Van Helsing) and Herbert Bunston (as Dr. Seward) would reprise their roles from the Broadway production. Finally, actress Helen Chandler was cast as Mina Seward, the object of the Count's affection. But without Chaney, the movie was missing someone with star power. To make matters worse, the film's budget was nearly drained. Whoever was chosen to play the Count would have to work for a measly sum.

After considering a number of actors to play the lead, Universal decided to hire Bela Lugosi, who was coming off a successful run as the Count on Broadway. No one knew the character of Count Dracula as well as Lugosi. Furthermore, he would work for the paltry sum of $3,500. Little did anyone know at the time that Lugosi's portrayal of Count Dracula would become one of the most memorable roles in the history of cinema.

Filming began on September 29, 1930, and wrapped on November 15, 1930, two weeks early, but $14,000 over-budget. The filming took place at Universal's enormous back lot, a place made famous for bringing other worlds to life on the silver screen.

During the shooting of *Dracula*, a Spanish movie company filmed a very similar picture. While Browning and his crew would work during the day, the Spanish company would come in and shoot all night, using the same sets and props. However, an entirely new cast and crew were used. Many film historians believe the Spanish version to be far superior to Browning's film.

PUBLIC REACTION

Dracula premiered on February 13, 1931, at the Roxy Theater in New York City. The film was introduced around the city with a grisly advertising campaign. Movie posters featured bloodlike paint, and Bela Lugosi's ghostly image haunted the city.

When the movie premiered, New York press reaction to the film was mixed at best. Some critics found the film exciting and mesmerizing, while others found it slow and inconsistent. The mixed reviews slowed the public reaction to the film, and *Dracula* closed at the Roxy after only eight days. But *Dracula* went national a month later, and excitement for the film began to grow. Theaters showed the film at special midnight showings. Promoters used odd gimmicks to attract fans. (One promoter in Detroit, Michigan, actually released live bats into the theater!) The film's popularity slowly gained momentum over the year and, by the end of 1931, *Dracula* would be Universal's top moneymaker.

CRITICAL REACTION

Although the public was hypnotized by the Count, movie historians criticize *Dracula* for being flawed in many areas, for many production details were overlooked. If you look closely at some scenes, props and technical hardware are left in the shot. In addition, the film has some rather odd choices of imagery, such as the use of armadillos crawling around during the scenes inside Dracula's castle.

Another criticism was the work of the director. Browning had made his reputation in silent films. With the dawn of "talkies," Browning was out of place. At times, the dialogue is bogged down, at others, there are long moments of silence. Browning also cut many key shots from the original script that may have greatly improved the movie. Critics also say that Browning relied too heavily on long shots when close-ups would have been more effective, and that he let scenes run too long without cutting to different camera angles. Most critics agree that the first half of the movie is far superior to the second half. It was almost as if the director had lost interest in the film as production went along.

Compared with Lugosi's performance, the other actors were underutilized and fairly dull onscreen. The movie's second-best performance was Dwight Frye's role as the Count's demented assistant, Renfield. Like Lugosi, Frye would eventually be typecast. His next great role was as Dr. Frankenstein's hunchbacked assistant in *Frankenstein*.

Despite these problems, *Dracula* was groundbreaking in many areas. Cinematographer Karl Freund used multiple cameras along with moving-camera shots, two things never successfully used in film before. The film also utilized Universal's resources to create memorable sets. The scenes inside Dracula's castle are dazzling, filled with Gothic architecture and the heightened atmosphere of a horror movie. Although it may not be a flawless movie, *Dracula* contains certain scenes that remain some of the most impressive in film history.

CHAPTER 3

MYTH OF THE VAMPIRE

The Count Dracula we are familiar with today came directly from Bram Stoker's 1897 novel *Dracula*. However, dark tales of vampires existed for hundreds of years before Stoker's novel was even published.

As do many of today's legendary film monsters, *Dracula* has deep roots in folklore and legend of old Europe and Asia. Many of these stories had religious undertones, where the vampire represented the evils and mysteries of sin and life beyond the grave. Vampires were widely considered to be creatures that return from the dead to drain the blood or energy from the living. The description of these creatures varied from culture to culture. In the Far East, they appeared as zombielike creatures with pink hair. As the centuries passed, the vampire myth moved west and into eastern Europe where it transformed itself into the myths we know today.

SLAVIC VAMPIRES

The vampires of eastern Europe first emerged around the eighth century AD in

Slavic countries such as Russia, Bulgaria, Poland, and Romania. At the time, Christianity was fighting for dominance over Europe. Here, the vampire legend began to immerse itself in religion, as Christians used the dark beings to help explain the unexplainable. Possible causes of vampirism began to arise as part of this folklore. Some of the explanations for vampirism included being conceived on certain days or being improperly buried. Likewise, rules for preventing people from becoming vampires, or killing them once they did, also began to arise. These legends included placing a cross in the coffin of the dead, tacking the dead person's clothes to the coffin, or piercing the body with thorns or stakes. Some of these beliefs continued with the modern legend of the vampire.

ROMANIAN VAMPIRES

The eastern European country of Romania is home to many of the vampire legends we are familiar with today. Romania is a vast country that stands as a last outpost before Europe gives way to Asia. Romania is also home to the province of Transylvania, the traditional home of Count Dracula.

The Romanians developed many causes for being damned to vampirism. These causes included being born out of wedlock, dying before baptism, being born as the seventh child, or, of course, being bitten by an existing vampire. To kill a vampire, the Romanians believed, one must drive a stake through its body, decapitate the corpse, and stuff the mouth full of garlic. Many of these Romanian beliefs would be used in Bram Stoker's famous novel.

VAMPIRES IN VICTORIAN ENGLAND

Vampire tales in literature began appearing in France and England in the early nineteenth century. Englishman Dr. John Polidori first popularized the English vampire tale in his 1819 novel, *The Vampyre*. Several versions of the vampire story followed, most notably, Joseph Sheridan Le Fanu's 1871 novella, *Carmilla*. This piece would have a profound influence on a young Irishman named Bram Stoker.

Shown above is an illustration from *Varney the Vampire or the Feast of Blood*, a penny dreadful circa 1800. The term "penny dreadful" was used to describe violent crime or adventure novels. Vampire stories were popular in nineteenth-century literature. These tales inspired young Bram Stoker.

BRAM STOKER'S *DRACULA*

Bram Stoker was born in Dublin, Ireland, in 1847, and suffered through a sickly childhood. As a young man, Stoker was inspired by Le Fanu's tales. By his early twenties, Stoker had embarked on a writing career of his own.

In 1875, Stoker published his first set of horror tales entitled *The Chain of Destiny*. As his writing career began,

Pictured are the ruins of Princely Court, the home of Vlad Dracula, located in Tirgoviste, Romania. Vlad Dracula, also known as Vlad the Impaler, was the real-life inspiration for the Count Dracula made famous in Bram Stoker's novel. Though he did not suck the blood out of his victims, his reign as ruler of Wallachia, a Romanian province, was a bloody one in which he became famous for impaling his enemies.

Stoker took a job writing theater reviews for the *Dublin Mail*. During this time, he befriended the acclaimed stage actor Sir Henry Irving. In 1878, Stoker took over managing Irving's stage company, the London Lyceum. Here, Stoker would find the passion and inspiration to begin work on his greatest tale.

In the early 1890s, Stoker began work on his masterpiece, originally entitled *The Un-Dead*. The novel was finally published as *Dracula* in 1897 and almost immediately cast a spell over the reading public. The novel uses an epistolary narrative device, which weaves a series of diary and journal entries from the main characters. This narrative allows the reader to get inside the mind of each character as the story unfolds and the characters realize the horror they are facing—the horror that Count Dracula the vampire is walking among them. The story took several years to write and went through many changes. One such change was Stoker's original name for his vampire—Count Vampyre. Then the author discovered a little-known histori-cal figure, Vlad the Impaler.

This photograph of Bram Stoker was taken around 1900. The Irishman wrote many novels, short stories, and essays, but he is most famous for *Dracula*. Though numerous writers since Stoker have expanded the vampire myth, they have all been influenced by his work.

Stoker's novel dove deeply into the psyche of Victorian England. To this day, scholars argue over the purpose of Stoker's work. Some say it was a religious allegory of cultural paranoia that evils were encroaching on Christian Europe. Others say that the book was a look into the darker aspects of the human mind.

VLAD TEPES: THE REAL DRACULA?

Today, most of the vampires we see in the movies draw their inspiration from Stoker's book. But Stoker himself needed inspiration to create his Dark Prince. He found this inspiration in a minor fifteenth-century Romanian ruler named Vlad Tepes, better known as Vlad the Impaler. Vlad would have become a minor footnote in European history if it were not for Stoker's book. Today Vlad the Impaler is thought of as the "real" Count Dracula.

Vlad Tepes was born in 1431 and later ruled over a Romanian province called Wallachia, near Transylvania. Although Vlad the Impaler was not the blood-sucking vampire we see in movies, he did have a taste for blood.

At the time, Romania stood as the outpost that defended Christian Europe from Islam in the Middle East. Vlad followed in his father's footsteps as a passionate defender of Christianity. When the Islamic Turks killed his father, Vlad became vengeful and his reign became bloody. After killing his enemies, Vlad would impale their bodies on stakes surrounding his castle. Sometimes his enemies were impaled while still alive, which led to a very slow and painful death. According to legend, Vlad the Impaler was known to set up a banquet and dine around his victims.

But the connection to Stoker's Count Dracula does not stop there. Vlad's father, also named Vlad, belonged to the Order of the Dragon. This organization of the Roman Catholic Church was dedicated to destroying rivals in eastern Europe. From the Order of the Dragon, the elder Vlad adopted the name Dracul, which means "dragon" or "devil" in Romanian. Hence, his son would adopt the name Dracula, with the "a" added to show lineage.

Ultimately, Vlad the Impaler's short yet bloody reign got the best of him. He was overthrown twice and was eventually killed by one of his own subjects. Nearly 400 years later, Stoker would raise Vlad the Impaler from the dead and immortalize him within the pages of the chilling *Dracula*.

Whatever Stoker's reasons for writing *Dracula*, the book had an immediate impact on the general public. As soon as word spread through the country about this dark and chilling new novel, Stoker and others began to realize the theatrical value of his tale. The legend of Dracula would soon leave the pages of a novel and begin to be portrayed in dramatic readings, on the theatrical stage, and eventually on film. Stoker himself would not see the potential of his tale realized. Stoker died in 1912, leaving behind one of the most important books of the late nineteenth century. His work would also stand as the ultimate authority on the vampire tale, where his characters would be re-created repeatedly to weave the wicked tale of Count Dracula.

CHAPTER 4

THE LEGEND OF COUNT DRACULA

The success of *Dracula* led to an explosion in monster movies, especially at Universal Studios. Set designers at Universal mastered the art of producing the feel of a horror movie. They created signature sets, where trees twisted and turned into terrifying shapes, and dark, Gothic buildings cast the scene in shadow.

In 1931, Universal also released *Frankenstein*, a movie that equaled the popularity of *Dracula*. *Frankenstein* even spawned a star with popularity equal to that of Bela Lugosi. Boris Karloff played Dr. Frankenstein's monster and became an instant sensation.

Also released in 1931, *Dr. Jekyll and Mr. Hyde* would enthrall moviegoers. The following year Universal released *The Mummy*, also starring Karloff. Like *Dracula*, both *Frankenstein* and *The Mummy* generated several spin-offs. In 1933, another giant of the monster-movie genre would arrive in *King Kong*. By then there was no denying the growing popularity of the movie monster.

Actors Irving Pichel and Gloria Holden are featured in a still from *Dracula's Daughter* (1936), a sequel to *Dracula*. The 1930s saw a host of monster movies following on the success of films like *Dracula* and *King Kong*. Audiences flocked to these movies, but the outbreak of World War II in 1939 put a temporary stop to the genre.

THE DRACULA INDUSTRY BEGINS

In 1936, Universal released its first follow-up to *Dracula*, hoping to cash in on the original movie's success. The studio initially planned *Dracula's Daughter* to be based on Bram Stoker's short story, *Dracula's Guest*. However, more contract disputes inside the studio turned the movie into a completely unrelated story. *Dracula's Daughter* acted as a direct sequel to

Dracula, beginning right where the original left off. Professor Van Helsing has just staked the body of Count Dracula. The body is then taken to the morgue where it vanishes. Soon, an exotic beauty arrives, seemingly under the spell of the late Count, and the city is once again plunged into fear as drained bodies begin appearing. The movie was both a critical and box-office success.

By the late 1930s, it looked as though nothing could slow the popularity of monster movies. Nevertheless, in 1939, America's horror industry came to a screeching halt. Great Britain ordered an embargo, or stoppage, on importing American horror movies during World War II (1939–1945), fearing they would reduce the morale of the English people. This had a serious impact on movie studios, which quickly moved away from producing horror films. But the popularity of the monster movie could not be suppressed for long. In 1941, *The Wolf Man* starring Lon Chaney Jr., son of the legendary actor, was released to rave reviews. The monster movie was back.

THE 1940S

During the 1940s, the horror movie would establish itself as a movie genre that was here to stay. In 1943, Universal's second *Dracula* follow-up appeared in the form of *Son of Dracula*. The movie starred Lon Chaney Jr. Chaney's performance is memorable as the menacing vampire who returns to haunt England in his father's footsteps.

In 1944, Universal released *House of Frankenstein*. The movie was an odd mix, capitalizing on popular monsters with monster team-ups. Boris Karloff, who rose to fame playing Frankenstein's monster, played the imprisoned Dr. Gustav Niemann. In this film, Dr. Niemann escapes from prison to resurrect the body of Count Dracula. Even the Wolf Man gets involved, as Lon Chaney Jr. revives his classic werewolf role. However strange the movie was, it was extremely popular with the public. Today it is considered a classic horror film. The following year would greet another classic monster team-up film in *House of Dracula*. This time, the Count and the Wolf Man teamed up to terrorize innocent city dwellers.

Bela Lugosi (*right*), shown here with Lou Costello, reprised his role as Dracula for *Abbott and Costello Meet Frankenstein*, a parody of monster movies in which the comedy team squares off with Dracula and Frankenstein's monster.

By now, the monster movie was turning into a parody of itself. This would be confirmed in the 1948 classic comedy *Abbott and Costello Meet Frankenstein*. Bud Abbott and Lou Costello made up the most popular comedy duo of their time. For this movie, Abbott and Costello would meet their match with the monster duo of Count Dracula and Frankenstein's monster. It was an odd collision of universes. But the result was a

Christopher Lee starred in countless vampire movies in the 1960s. However, unlike Bela Lugosi, Lee was able to escape the typecasting normally associated with the role of Dracula. He forged a versatile career in Hollywood, appearing in such recent films as *Sleepy Hollow* (1999), *Star Wars: Episode II* (2002), the *Lord of the Rings* trilogy, and *Charlie and the Chocolate Factory* (2005).

smashing success. The film starred Bela Lugosi as Count Dracula, Glenn Strange as Frankenstein's monster, and Lon Chaney Jr. as the Wolf Man. Abbott and Costello would go on to film several other monster movies, such as *Abbott and Costello Meet the Invisible Man* (1951) and *Abbott and Costello Meet the Mummy* (1955).

HAMMER FILMS

By the mid-1950s, Count Dracula was big business. In 1958, Hammer Films, a British studio, released its first of eight movies based on the Dracula character. *The Horror of Dracula* appeared in Technicolor, an early version of color film. The movie captured the blood and gore of the vampire tale and was a resounding success. The film starred a young and upcoming actor named Christopher Lee as the Count. Lee would star in several more Hammer movies and establish himself as the new king of vampire movies. Lee would go on to star in *Dracula, Prince of Darkness* (1966) and *Dracula Has Risen from the Grave* (1968), among others. Unlike Lugosi, however, Lee was able to escape the shadow of Count Dracula and establish a long and successful acting career. Most recently, he played the evil Saruman in the *Lord of the Rings* trilogy and Darth Tyranus/Count Dooku in director George Lucas's *Star Wars: Episode II*.

THE 1960S AND BEYOND

In the 1960s, the horror-movie genre tightened its grip on American youth as a giant subculture of fans emerged. Television also emerged as a popular new medium. Across the country, television stations regularly aired horror movies as part of afternoon shows like *Creature Feature*. The shows were often hosted by wacky characters such as Vampira in Los Angeles and Zacherley in New York City. These shows allowed classic monster movies to be introduced to a whole

Gary Oldman starred as Dracula and Winona Ryder as Mina in *Bram Stoker's Dracula* (1992), director Francis Ford Coppola's imagining of the vampire tale. The movie was a critical and financial success and is considered the most faithful screen adaptation of Stoker's novel.

new generation of fans. Likewise, horror comics and magazines for adolescents sprang up, filled with twisted tales of terror. Count Dracula, of course, was a favorite character.

This zealous interest in Dracula and vampires in general not only brought forth the series of Hammer Films, but several parodies of the Count. Some of the more notable parodies included *Billy the Kid Versus Dracula* (1966), *Dracula Meets the Outer Space Chicks* (1968), the "blaxploitation" film *Blacula* (1972), and *Andy Warhol's Dracula* (1974), the strange art film directed by the great American pop artist.

In 1979, Universal produced an updated version of *Dracula*. This time the film starred the dashing Frank Langella, who was fresh from a successful run playing the lead role in *Dracula* on Broadway. The Van Helsing role was played by the renowned actor Sir Laurence Olivier. The movie was a major production and was moderately successful with both the public and the critics.

Bela Lugosi Jr. poses with a painting of his father to celebrate the 1997 release of a series of U.S. postage stamps honoring actors who portrayed famous movie monsters. Other actors such as Lon Chaney, Boris Karloff, and Lon Chaney Jr. were also honored with stamps.

The most recent great Dracula-inspired movie was 1992's *Bram Stoker's Dracula*, directed by acclaimed director Francis Ford Coppola. Out of all the Dracula movies, this version is closest to Stoker's novel. The movie is a spectacle in itself, starring Anthony Hopkins as Van Helsing, Gary Oldman as Dracula, and Keanu Reeves as Jonathan Harker. The movie

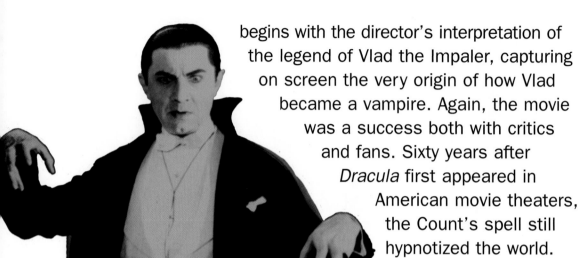

begins with the director's interpretation of the legend of Vlad the Impaler, capturing on screen the very origin of how Vlad became a vampire. Again, the movie was a success both with critics and fans. Sixty years after *Dracula* first appeared in American movie theaters, the Count's spell still hypnotized the world.

The legend of Count Dracula continues to grow to this day. The world holds tight to its fascination with vampires and the undead. Author Anne Rice published a series of wildly popular

Many films have come and gone since *Dracula*, but Bela Lugosi's portrayal of the Count remains the definitive vampire performance.

vampire tales beginning in the 1970s (one book in the series was turned into the movie *Interview with the Vampire* starring Brad Pitt and Tom Cruise). Television shows such as *Buffy the Vampire Slayer* and *Angel* capture the allure of the vampire myth and pair it with the trials of growing up in the modern world. Every year sees new versions of the vampire myth in books, television, and movies. Even New York's Broadway renewed its fascination with the Count in its August 2004 production of *Dracula, the Musical* at the Balasco Theatre. The original Dracula might be dead, but his legend lives on.

FILMOGRAPHY

Nosferatu (1922) German film studio Prana Films produces the first great Dracula movie, all but stealing the storyline from Stoker's novel.

Dracula (1931) Debuts at the Roxy Theater in New York on Friday, February 13. Bela Lugosi rises to stardom.

Dracula's Daughter (1936) A direct sequel to the original as Universal attempts to cash in on the popularity of vampires.

House of Frankenstein (1944) The first of several monster team-up movies released by Universal.

House of Dracula (1945) The second of Universal's monster team-ups starring the Count.

Abbott and Costello Meet Frankenstein (1948) The smash-hit comedy marks the last time Bela Lugosi will play Count Dracula on film.

The Horror of Dracula (1958) Hammer Films releases its first of several bloody gothic-inspired Dracula films starring Christopher Lee.

The Brides of Dracula (1960) Another Hammer Films horror flick. Despite the film's title, there is no Count Dracula character in the movie.

Dracula, Prince of Darkness (1966) Possibly the finest of the Dracula-based Hammer Films starring Christopher Lee.

Dracula Has Risen from the Grave (1968) Christopher Lee reprises his role as the Count.

Dracula Meets the Outer Space Chicks (1968) The first of many silly Dracula parodies.

Blacula (1972) This classic "blaxploitation" film revolves around a Count from the Caribbean.

Dracula AD 1972 (1972) Christopher Lee returns once again in this Hammer production.

Andy Warhol's Dracula (1973) The great New York City pop artist releases his take on the vampire tale.

The Satanic Rites of Dracula (1973) Christopher Lee plays the Count for the eighth and final time.

Count Dracula (1978) The British Broadcasting Company (BBC) releases this stunning miniseries, one of the best and most-faithful retellings of Stoker's tale.

Dracula (1979) Universal releases the moderately successful updated version starring Frank Langella and Sir Laurence Olivier.

Bram Stoker's Dracula (1992) Very successful at the box office, the film is directed by Francis Ford Coppola and stars Gary Oldman as the Count.

Van Helsing (2004) Hugh Jackman stars in this action picture following the legendary vampire hunter.

GLOSSARY

allegory Using fictional characters and stories to understand truths and generalizations in life.

baptism Religious ceremony that symbolizes acceptance into the Christian community.

blaxploitation The exploitation of blacks by producers of black-oriented films.

B movies Poorly made, low-budget movies.

conceive To become pregnant.

epistolary narrative Story told through journals, diaries, and letters.

impale To pierce with something pointed.

lineage A group with common ancestors.

morale Sense of loyalty or enthusiasm.

novella A work of fiction that falls in length and complexity between a short story and a novel.

parody Imitate for comic effect.

reign The time that someone rules over others.

vengeful Seeking to punish a wrongdoer.

FOR MORE INFORMATION

American Film Institute
2021 N. Western Avenue
Los Angeles, CA 90027-1657
(323) 856-7600
Web site: http://www.afi.com

WEB SITES

Due to the changing nature of Internet links, the Rosen
Publishing Group, Inc., has developed an online list of Web
sites related to the subject of this book. This site is updated
regularly. Please use this link to access the list:

http://www.rosenlinks.com/famm/medr

FOR FURTHER READING AND VIEWING

BOOKS

Joslin, Lyndon W. *Count Dracula Goes to the Movies: Stoker's Novel Adapted, 1922–1995*. Jefferson, NC: McFarland & Co., 1999.

McNally, Raymond T., and Radu R. Florescu. *In Search of Dracula: The History of Dracula and Vampires*. Boston: Houghton Mifflin, 1994.

Melton, J. Gordon. *The Vampire Book: The Encyclopedia of the Undead*. Detroit: Visible Ink Press, 1994.

Skal, David J. *Hollywood Gothic*. New York: W. W. Norton & Co., 1990.

Stoker, Bram. *Dracula*. New York: Penguin Classics, 2003.

MOVIES

Bram Stoker's Dracula, directed by Francis Ford Coppola. Columbia/TriStar Studios, 1992. DVD.

Dracula, directed by John Badham. Image Studios, 1979. DVD.

Dracula, directed by Tod Browning. Universal Studios, 1931. DVD.

Dracula (also known as *The Horror of Dracula*), directed by Terence Fisher. Hammer Films, 1958. DVD.

Nosferatu—Special Edition, directed by F. W. Murnau. Image Entertainment, 1922. DVD.

BIBLIOGRAPHY

Carroll, David, and Kyla Ward. "The Horror Timeline: Early 20th Century." Tabula Rasa. Retrieved February 2004 (http://www.tabula-rasa.info/DarkAges/Timeline2.html).

Holte, James Craig. *Dracula in the Dark*. Westport, CT: Greenwood Press, 1997.

Melton, J. Gordon. *The Vampire Book: The Encyclopedia of the Undead*. Detroit: Visible Ink Press, 1994.

Skal, David J. *Hollywood Gothic.* New York: W. W. Norton & Co., 1990.

Walker, Gregory A. *The Living and the Undead.* Urbana, IL: University of Illinois Press, 1986.

INDEX

ABOUT THE AUTHOR

Charles Hofer is a writer and editor who lives in Brooklyn, New York.

PHOTO CREDITS

Cover, p. 1 © Underwood and Underwood/Corbis; illustration p. 1 by Thomas Forget; pp. 4, 9, 14, 15, 18, 19, 21, 25, 29, 32, 35 © Bettmann/Corbis; pp. 5, 16, 38 © The Everett Collection; p. 10 © John Springer Collection/Corbis; pp. 27, 30, 33, 36 © Hulton/Archive/Getty Images, Inc.; p. 28 © Janet Wishnetsky/Corbis; pp. 39, 40 © AP/Wide World Photos.

Designer: Thomas Forget; Editor: Kathy Kuhtz Campbell